SO-AIP-454

POETRY
SECTION

The

Last

Uncle

Also by LINDA PASTAN

The

Last

Uncle

LINDA PASTAN

W · W · NORTON & COMPANY
NEW YORK · LONDON

Copyright © 2002 by Linda Pastan

For information about permission to reproduce selections from this book, write to
Permissions, W. W. Norton & Company, Inc., 500 Fifth Avenue, New York, NY 10110

The text of this book is composed in New Caledonia with the display set in Bulmar
Composition by Adrian Kitzinger
Manufacturing by Courier Westford
Production manager: Julia Druskin

Library of Congress Cataloging-in-Publication Data

Pastan, Linda, 1932–
    The last uncle : [poems] / by Linda Pastan.
      p. cm.
    ISBN 0-393-05063-7
      I. Title.

PS3566.A775 L37 2002
811'.54—dc21   2001055751

W. W. Norton & Company, Inc., 500 Fifth Avenue, New York, N.Y. 10110
www.wwnorton.com

W. W. Norton & Company Ltd., Castle House, 75/76 Wells Street, London W1T 3QT

1 2 3 4 5 6 7 8 9 0

for Amy, David, and Elizabeth

Contents

3.

4.

5.

Acknowledgments

I would like to thank the following magazines in which many of these poems first appeared:

The Cider Press, 5 Points, The Gettysburg Review, The Georgia Review, The Great River Review, The Kenyon Review, The Ohio Review, The Paris Review, Pivot, Ploughshares, Poetry, Prairie Schooner, Princeton University Library Chronicles, River City, The Virginia Quarterly Review

1.

"Women on the Shore"

The pills I take to postpone death
are killing me, and the healing
journey we pack for waits
with its broken airplane,
the malarial hum of mosquitos.
Even the newly mowed domestic grass
hides fault lines in the earth
which could open at any time

and swallow us.
In Edvard Munch's woodcut,
the pure geometry of color—an arctic sky,
the luminescent blues and greens of water—
surrounds the woman in black
whose head is turning to a skull.
If death is everywhere we look,
at least let's marry it to beauty.

Practicing

My son is practicing the piano.
He is a man now, not the boy
whose lessons I once sat through,
whose reluctant practicing
I demanded—part of the obligation
I felt to the growth
and composition of a child.

Upstairs my grandchildren are sleeping,
though they complained earlier of the music
which rises like smoke up through the floorboards,
coloring the fabric of their dreams.
On the porch my husband watches the garden fade
into summer twilight, flower by flower;
it must be a little like listening to the fading

diminuendo notes of Mozart.
But here where the dining room table
has been pushed aside to make room
for this second or third-hand upright,
my son is playing the kind of music
it took him all these years,
and sons of his own, to want to make.

Muse

after reading Rilke

No angel speaks to me.
And though the wind
plucks the dry leaves
as if they were so many notes
of music, I can hear no words.

Still, I listen. I search
the feathery shapes of clouds
hoping to find the curve of a wing.
And sometimes, when the static
of the world clears just for a moment

a small voice comes through,
chastening. Music
is its own language, it says.
Along the indifferent corridors
of space, angels could be hiding.

Tears

"Save us from tears that bring no healing . . ."
—MATTHEW ARNOLD

When the ophthalmologist told me gravely
that I didn't produce enough tears,
I wanted to say: but I cry too much
and too often. At airports and weddings
and sunsets. At movies

where the swell of sentimental music
forces open my tear ducts
like so many locks in a canal.
And when he handed me this vial
of artificial tears, I wanted to tell him

about Niobe. Perhaps if her tear ducts
had been deficient, she wouldn't
have dissolved into salty water
after the loss of her children.
Maybe other heroes and heroines

deprived of the resonant ability to cry
would have picked themselves up
and acted sensibly. Othello for instance
who wept, before he killed her,
into Desdemona's embroidered pillow.

And so I take this bottle of distilled grief
and put it in the back of a drawer,
but I don't throw it away. There may be poems
in the future that need to be watered,
for I still remember Tennyson

who wrote of how short swallow-flights of song
dip their wings in tears, and skim away.

6

A Glass of Cold Water

Poetry is not a code
to be broken
but a way of seeing
with the eyes shut,
of short-
circuiting the usual
connections until
lioness and
knee become
the same thing.

Though not a cure
it can console,
the way cool sheets
console
the dying flesh,
the way a glass of cold
water can be
a way station
on the unswerving
road to thirst.

To a Poet, Recently Silent

1.

Have you run out
of words?
Like this tree
which relinquished
its bronzed leaves
one by one, have you
used up everything
you had to say?
Or is your silence
music in the mouth
of someone
who has simply decided
not to sing?

2.

Syllables and years
in old and stringent patterns
both run out so soon.

3.

In Monet's *Studio Boat*,
which you sent us to see,
the unresolved shadow
in the bow could be you,
writing your poems in perfect
privacy, then sending the dark
words floating down the Seine
to be washed in water
until they shine like fish scales.

Austerity

If I had to live
my life again,
I would work only
in black and white.
I remember Degas's words
as the snow continues
to fall, blanking out
the green earth,
bleaching the sky,
until only the black
shadows of buildings
are left and the wet trunks
of trees, darkened
with cold.
This is the death
of color. Winter
is slamming its door
on the heart, and soon
nothing will remain
but beauty—
the austere line
of charcoal moving
across white paper,
of bootprints engraved
upon new snow.

The Invalid

You lie spread-eagled on the bed
like Leonardo's study of anatomy,
your navel the proven center of the universe,
the scattered pills on your blanket
as shiny as anonymous stars.

This is less than life, you think,
though surely more than death,
a stopping-off place
between matter and energy.
For though your symptoms languish

from week to week, the road
to recovery leads always back
to this place, this bed, as if you were
a 19th century poetess, wedded
to your chaise lounge,

a small black dog tucked
into the curve of an arm as pale
as any breast, and belladonna
making your eyes unfathomable
as one of your fevered poems.

Death of a Potter

for Vally

When her wheel suddenly
stopped turning, a round world
was stilled on its axis,

and where her hands had shaped
so many forms in air—
throwing, they call it—

there would be emptiness.
Today rain glazes the flowers;
shards of winter linger here.

They place her in the kiln of earth,
where clay is fired until
the bones shine like porcelain.

The Answering Machine

I call and hear your voice
on the answering machine
weeks after your death,
a fledgling ghost still longing
for human messages.

Shall I leave one, telling
how the fabric of our lives
has been ripped before
but that this sudden tear will not
be mended soon or easily?

In your emptying house, others
roll up rugs, pack books,
drink coffee at your antique table,
and listen to messages left
on a machine haunted

by the timbre of your voice,
more palpable than photographs
or fingerprints. On this first day
of this first fall without you,
ashamed and resisting

but compelled, I dial again
the number I know by heart,
thankful in a diminished world
for the accidental mercy of machines,
then listen and hang up.

Grace

When the young professor folded
his hands at dinner and spoke to God
about my safe arrival
through the snow, thanking Him also
for the food we were about to eat,

it was in the tone of voice I use
to speak to friends when I call
and get their answering machines,
chatting about this and that
in a casual voice,

picturing them listening
but too busy to pick up the phone,
or out taking care of important
business somewhere else.
The next day, flying home

through a windy
and overwhelming sky, I knew
I envied his rapport with God
and hoped his prayers
would keep my plane aloft.

The Dangerous Month of March

In the dangerous month of March,
when the daffodils use up their sulfurous firepower
and are cut down by a cunning wind,
when the doctors hand out their pills, their diagnoses,
their old, thumbed-over magazines, I return home
immune at last to the treacheries of weather.
I have turned off the phone;
now it is a mute animal squatting
on the gate-legged table. I have unscrewed
the door knocker—boneless knuckle,
pulled down the blinds, pleat
by pleat, and let the newspapers
gather on my doorstep like so much
foamy detritus on an empty beach.
Now I can be alone—no sorrow,
no news of death blowing its shrill
whistle as it approaches down the track,
no friend drowning in a rising tide
of cells. There is simply silence
and semi-darkness as I watch
make believe lives on the TV screen,
a great blue-lit pantomime
of life and love and death, reflecting
only the flickering shadows of pain.
Safe in the house, locked in, alone,
I can ignore the deer ravaging
the wild ginger, beauty devouring beauty.
I can ignore the voices of children
calling goodbye to their childhoods,
the voices of old women in black—
not the black of Sicilian grandmothers
but of Hollywood stars who long ago lost
their lustre and hide in the sophisticated clothes
they will be buried in soon, their coffins
strewn with resurrected daffodils.

The Cossacks

for F.

For Jews, the Cossacks are always coming.
Therefore I think the sun spot on my arm
is melanoma. Therefore I celebrate
New Year's Eve by counting
my annual dead.

My mother, when she was dying,
spoke to her visitors of books
and travel, displaying serenity
as a form of manners, though
I could tell the difference.

But when I watched you planning
for a life you knew
you'd never have, I couldn't explain
your genuine smile in the face
of disaster. Was it denial

laced with acceptance? Or was it
generations of being English—
Brontë's Lucy, in *Villette*
living as if no fire raged
beneath her dun-colored dress.

I want to live the way you did,
preparing for next year's famine with wine
and music as if it were a ten-course banquet.
But listen: those are hoofbeats
on the frosty autumn air.

2.

Memory's Guest

I am memory's guest.
Warmed at her fires,
half drowsing
in her flickering
shadow light, I hear
lost voices speak to me.

Outside leaves and blossoms
come and go, travellers
on the round trip
through the seasons,
their vivid world
is the dream

I must return to,
chastened but comforted.
For now, I am resting
on the flowery
cushions of the past.

Family History

My uncle changed
from Izzie to Irving
to Irvin, enroute
from the Lower East Side,
via Bush Street,
all the way
to Riverside Drive.

But now that his skull
is taking on
the luminous form
of his father's,
we hurry
to ask him all
the questions

we never thought
to ask before.
It is twilight, even here
in the suburbs.
He is the only
Herodotus
we have left.

Frances and Mary Allen, *Sewing Group*, ca. 1900

platinum print

The three fates in dark
skirts and starched shirtwaists
bend over their work,
tracing the abstract patterns
of our lives in small, neat stitches,
keeping their glittering scissors
just out of sight;

like my three great-aunts
dying slowly in their
New World tenement,
a fan of silver pins
in each of their
pursed mouths;

or the Allen sisters
in a trance of needles and thread,
the cloth spread out
like medieval finery
over their serious laps, the sky
outside the closed curtains
embroidered with those skeins of light
we still call stars.

The Lost Kingdom

"No book is as fictional as the one that begins I remember . . ."
—PATRICIA HAMPL

I remember the castle
and the chilly moat where we swam
or in winter skated,

and how on the shiny seat
of the coach an ermine lap robe
casually waited.

And all his courtiers smiled
and thanked him. I knew I was lucky
to be his daughter.

That was before the succession,
before the years had trickled through
my hands, like water.

March 5

March is the start
of the incontinent season.
My father would have been
one hundred today. Gone

for thirty years, but mysteries
still sprout like weeds
from his grave soil: his father
in America first, found

in a tenement with an extra wife;
my brother who never lived.
Beneath the scent
of Old Spice aftershave,

I remember a whiff
of steerage, of rotting fruit
from the Lower East Side,
the infamous restaurant.

Was it the sun reflected from
his cufflinks that made me blink,
or was I afraid to plumb the silence
of that house? Are leaves

simply indifferent
to the tree? I look at my aging
children. Ask me, I want
to tell them. Ask me now.

Reading the Obituary Page

In starched dresses
with ribbons
in miniature jackets
and tiny ties
we would circle
the chairs
at birthday parties and
when the music
stopped, lunge
to be seated. One
by one we were welcomed
to hard ground
and empty air.

Potsy

The cards that come each Christmas
bear signatures from another life.
I line them on the mantel in the kind of rows
we stood in for school pictures,
and the names are the same:
Lila so fleet of foot, the bobbles
on her socks like the wings
of Mercury as she ran; Rowena
playing potsy; Gerda with her braids
and budding irony—girls
I've lost, except at Christmastime,
whose voices once bloomed daily
on the phone (their numbers fixed
like music in my mind: Tremont 2
and Endicott 9). Sometimes I think
we keep in touch each year
so we will recognize each other
in the life to come, when we leave
our womanly disguises behind
and circle back to the past,
the way we did playing potsy
when we jumped from square
to square, ending
on square one where we began,
with daylight fading, though
we hardly noticed it, ignoring
our mothers who were calling us
to supper and our separate lives.

Bess

When Bess, the landlord's black-eyed
daughter, waited for her highwayman
in the poem I learned by breathless
heart at twelve, it occurred to me

for the first time that my mild-eyed
mother Bess might have a life
all her own—a secret past
I couldn't enter, except in dreams.

That single sigh of a syllable
has passed like a keepsake
to this newest child, wrapped now
in the silence of sleep.

And in the dream I enter,
I could be holding my infant mother
in my arms: the same wide cheekbones,
the name indelible as a birthmark.

Armonk

In sleep I summon it—dark green shutters
opening on my childhood, white clapboards
bathed in the purple shadows
of azaleas, the perfect 18th century
farmhouse—"Armonk" we called it,
as if there were no village of that name.
How we loved the old, contorted apple trees
of Armonk, the revolutionary musket
in all its ornamental firepower hanging
over our mantel, the plain pine furniture
assembled from a more strictly crafted age.
It was as though we longed to be part
of a history that could replace our own
ancestors' broken nights in the shtetl
with the softly breaking light
of an American morning.

But what is history if not the imagination
of descendants, made almost flesh?
In old photographs, the cook holds high
a platter of Thanksgiving turkey,
an aunt waves from a mullioned window,
my mother, at her needle and thread, smiles
her understated smile. This
is my authentic childhood.
And my Orthodox grandfather, hunched
over a table, dealing out cards
in an endless game of pinochle,
straightens up for the camera.
Patriarch of the armchair, he could be
some early New England governor
posing for posterity in his starched
white shirt and dark cravat.

Another Autumn

Another autumn, the dogwoods turning first,
their hard berries bright as drops of blood
in the oak woods where a wild fox limped past
just yesterday—a harsher bleeding, and the sound of hounds
came faint as a scent on the wind, barred I had thought
from this wilderness of suburbs. I looked out
my kitchen window this morning and saw a deer,
tame as some neighbor's dog, eating the rhododendrons,
and I listened for the small thunder of shotguns
to stop that beautiful, omnivorous mouth.

The cold will come on fast now. Last week
I emptied the closet of its summer dresses;
draped over my arms they were pale
and insubstantial as last spring's flowers,
and the wool sweaters and skirts I hung in their place
depressed me with their heaviness, their dull, nut colors.
This is the true start of the year; the Jewish calendar
knows it, the school calendar too. Maybe that's why
our old dreams come back to taunt us, hanging
before our faces like condensed breath on this chilly air.

My parents married in fall, a May/September union.
Now in the crystalline light of that anniversary
the same questions repeat their old refrains.
Was love enough, even then?
Will we survive another winter? I remember
how my mother in her middle age looked
at my father, knowing he would be the first to go,
and how I looked at her, the last autumn of her life,
wanting her to flee that ravished flesh
but willing her to stay.

The Last Uncle

The last uncle is pushing off
in his funeral skiff (the usual
black limo) having locked
the doors behind him
on a whole generation.

And look, we are the elders now
with our torn scraps
of history, alone
on the mapless shore
of this raw, new century.

3.

Penultimate Things

Wearing their formal clothes,
their serious, funereal expressions

the last things of our lives prepare
their final speeches.

While they are busy, let me praise
penultimate things:

the bent branch
outside my window,

due to be kindling
next fall;

the car I taught my next to last
child to drive on,

rusting back
to its elements;

the 8th dog of my life;
the 10th scribbled book.

And love turning its back on endings
one more time.

Weather

Because of the menace
your father opened
like a black umbrella
and held high
over your childhood
blocking the light,
your life now seems

to you exceptional
in its simplicities.
You speak of this,
throwing the window open
on a plain spring day,
dazzling
after such a winter.

Husbandry

You move the sprinkler
from green to deeper green,
from threads of grass to
pin cushions of moss,

walking among your young plants
like the Creator himself
inventing rain,
or like the recluse artist

Ni Tsan who left his cave
to wash the paulownia trees
by hand, as if they were
his children.

Late Love Songs

1. Clerestory

Because, like the sun,
happiness can blind
when stared at
with the naked eye,
I have learned
to avert my face
partway

from certain
pleasures. They flood
the body anyhow,
as sunlight floods
our clerestory window
this morning, and lights
the entire room.

2. March Haiku

White petals, not snow,
fall improbably down on
our winter picnic.

3. Floodplain

In this strange spring—
cherry and dogwood blossoms overlapped
for the first time, forsythia
like electric lights left on too long—
I am as overwrought as the colors
in this garden, a floodplain
of feeling after the long rains
of April, the hours of weeping
over nothing, as the trout lilies
with their spotted, oval leaves
take hold everywhere.

4. Envoi

In this brief space I practice
saying goodbye, sitting
at your empty desk where,
if forty years have made us
one flesh, your pen
will recognize my hand
as my hand knows the touch
of yours in dark theaters,
in all the dark places.

The Vanity of Names

When the house of flesh disappears
in an earthquake of its own making,
this house of wood and glass
will stay fixed in its landscape.
Rooms will be swept clean
of all memories. Doors will close.
Even the animal graves out back
will forget who planted the bones
and whether the flowering cherry was a sign
of mourning or renewal.
This house will continue to rest
on its wide floorboards, somnolent
under its heavy eaves. Generations
will come and go. Someone will surely
notice how the sun slants through
the small eastern window,
a blade of light each morning,
and spreads like a cat stretching
against the western panes of glass
each afternoon. The house
we built will enter
the dreams of other people,
and they too will simply be tenants
of their own brief moments here.
I know all this. But to acquiesce
is never easy. It is to love the unwritten future
almost as well as the fading past.
It is to relinquish the vanity of names
which are already disappearing
with every cleansing rain
from the stooped and rusting mailbox.

To Penelope

after reading Cavafy's "Ithaca"

Let the days pass slowly, in Ithaca.
Let there be many summer days
with their lingering, lemony scents,
with all the perfumes of the sea
pricking your fine nostrils.
Your stuccoed walls, so cool to the touch,
are much too thick for you to hear
the noisy suitors downstairs.
And without the mess and bother
of a man, the sheets of your bed will remain
as white as the morning sands
after the sea has smoothed them.
But never forget Odysseus.
Without him and his journey
the olive trees wouldn't seem bent
in a passion of longing; your loom
would have stayed unstrung, its music
lost on a wind that never was.
Let others applaud you
for what they call patience.
The sound of their hands clapping
will be no more than a small surf beating the shore,
and besides, you deserve applause.
For you are like a fine actress
who takes her bows modestly,
and no one would ever guess you were in love
with solitude. But again, remember:
though he must come back at last,
though you must open your arms
which have grown strong alone at their weaving,
without Odysseus and his journey
there would be no tapestried story.

43rd Anniversary

I am plotting our life again,
here at the start of what must be
its final act. I am choosing
new scenery: antique rugs and clocks;
new characters—even a dog with a wise head
to be a kind of emblem,
like the lamb in *The Fairy Queen*
which accompanied Una everywhere.

And what do you plan,
you who garden as zealously
as if a wall of roses, a stand
of fruit trees, named and tagged,
could blossom into footlights
illuminating the fundamental
darkness of the woods?
What an enigmatic dance

we have always done together,
like one of those Andalusian dances
when the woman stands
as if musing,
spine straight, perfectly still
while the man, improvising,
stamps his feet
as he circles that stillness.

White Lies

When I swore, then,
that I loved you, I wasn't sure
I meant it, though I mean it now.

And when you said "forever,"
you knew the future was
bearing down on us,

its brakes worn out,
completely out of control.
In love's unblinking perjury,

fact and fiction smile
and embrace—
identical twins,

separated at birth.
You say I still look beautiful.
I say we'll always be together.

Round the Mulberry Bush

Monday

washing
Washday. Hum
of the Maytag swirling
its cocktail of clothes
as I sit idly, sipping my coffee.
Through the round porthole
I can see foamy water
and almost glimpse
the elbow of a woman
scrubbing her soiled clothes
in the rocky streambed
of another century.

Tuesday

ironing
Shaped like the perfect
bookend, my steam iron
waits in semi-retirement
in this house of wash and wear.
Sometimes I take it down (sizzle
of the afterworld) and slide it
across a single pillowslip,
my mother's white initial
a hidden watermark
at its embroidered hem.

Wednesday

sweeping
Commandant of the closet,
hank of straw lashed
to a long pole,
the new broom
pokes its head into
the corners and
under the marriage bed,
forgetting the dusty fields
it came from.

Thursday

darning
A lost art, like the painting
of the Czar's Easter egg
or the carving of a perfect
oval cameo.
My grandmother held
the wooden egg up to the light
as if it were a moon
and covered it with the cloud
of my grandfather's sock.

Friday

cleaning
Here I come, Mrs. Sisyphus
with my mops and dustpans,
my rags and Brillo pads.
I am the one who shovels snow
in the teeth of a blizzard
and tries to bail the ocean
out of a sinking boat
with a painted china teacup.

Saturday

baking
The dough swells
under its damp cloth
like an unborn child under
its mother's taut apron.
Smell of honey and
yeast, remembered whiff
of the afterbirth.
Later will come
the sharp knife,
the tearing
of bread like flesh.

Sunday

dressing up
I clothe myself
in silky blues
and greens, not to adorn
the Sabbath but
to make you remember
those moments
years ago, under
the mulberry bush.

4.

The Crossing

I wake to the small applause
of rain, then sleep again

and somewhere between dusk
and dawn a curtain falls and rises.

My dreams carry me
on their shifting backs

as if I were the round earth
balanced on the back of the tortoise

which pulls its head in now, safe and dry
within its perfect mosaic.

Listen: it is raining;
there is applause.

I must take my bows
and cross the swaying bridge, suspended

between sleep
and what is coming next.

Near the Sacrificial Site

Paestum, 1997

On an afternoon like this
I want permission to forget
the many varieties of cruelty.
I want the only figures of the past to be
ancestors of these wild
poppies, of this chestnut tree
whose blossoms break through
the hardest wood. I know that cruelty
flourishes just down the road, persistent
as these gnarled roots which overrun
the partly ruined woods.
But on an afternoon like this—
Old Master clouds and waterfalls of light—
I ask for the mercies of amnesia.
I want to open myself to the sun
which I know has killed
with its munificence,
to smell the foxglove
with no thought of the poison
hidden in its leaf.

We Get What We Wish For at Our Peril

On my 66th birthday, in rough winds
on the wrong Greek ferry—lost
and half a world from home,
I thought of Odysseus on these same
purpling, arrogant waters

and longed to be
Penelope again, lashed
to my loom and dreaming,
in the almond-scented
boredom of Ithaca.

Ghiaccio

At Herculaneum, where
steaming lava once crept
like a live and panting animal
over alleys and doorsteps, I fell
and broke my ankle. And lying
on the dusty ground, a tourist attraction
for passersby myself,
I wondered how, hobbled,
I would escape from lava or ash
or other more pedestrian dangers.
There is nothing like the sound
of bone cracking
to shift the axis of the earth,
and pain is never impersonal
but calls us by our given names.
In that ancient place, where the very sea
once fled its boundaries,
where antique human bones were found
heaped together—so many pieces
in an intricate puzzle now
but vulnerable once, and ordinary as mine,
I watched my ankle swell
to an unfamiliar, foreign shape;
and helpless, I tried to think
of the Italian word for ice.

Fibula

The muse has broken
her ankle too, the fibula.
She sits at the window
immobilized
and watches the trees
give up their color—
it's too much work just now
to chronicle the downward
twist of any leaf.
The muse muses on brittle
branches and bones;
she drinks her tea
in silence, sipping
the morning away, ignoring me.
Now she picks up a pencil—
her magic wand: "oh, the scarlet
canticles of autumn . . ."
Soon she puts it down again;
language is as hard
to master as crutches.

Wherever We Travel

Wherever we travel
it seems to take the same
few hours to get there.

The plane rises over clouds
into an unmarked sky,
comes down through clouds

to what we have to believe
is a different place. But here
are the same green road signs

the numbered highways
of home, with cars going
back and forth to houses

with chimneys and windows
identical to the ones we thought
we had left behind.

The radio blares familiar
radio music. Soon we will knock
on a door and someone will greet us,

will pull us into a room
we have never seen
but already know by heart.

Gone Missing

At the unmarked border
between sense
and senselessness
one boy steps over
the edge of the world
taking with him a blue
sweater, a razor, and
from the emptied pockets
of those he leaves behind
all certainty. The night

is very still, the only light
a cutting edge of moon.
He leaves his toothbrush,
the abstract letters of his name,
and a vision, photo perfect,
of what we fear the most:
our own loved children loosed
by stealth or accident
into the beautiful
and unforgiving world.

graffiti, route 22

the four-letter
words in glistening
spray paint
and the unrepentant
hearts with their
flagrant initials
on inaccessible
rocks
or the high
girders of bridges
call to us as we flash by,
in the acrobatic
hieroglyphics
of love

Crows

Like old Greek widows in black
head scarves and long, black skirts
gossiping at the well,

the crows hovered at the feeder
all morning, hunched together,
beaks touching.

When they finally took off
with a dark shuddering of wings,
the harsh caws rising

from those sleek black throats
cast a net of feathers
over the sun.

And though they were merely birds, not
prophetic women doling out luck
still, I was afraid.

Travelogue

I always take a book along,
raising it between my eyes and
whatever landscape I've come
so far to see—blue mountains,
or vineyards with their musky
purpling grapes; often a bay
or ocean unfolding just as far
as the horizon of the book
whose pages turn like surf
beneath my fingertips.

Perhaps I could simply stay at home
and have some cardboard scenery
shuffled at intervals. The story
I inhabit would be the same: a mystery
or poem, the memoir of some other
traveller in some other
more indelible century.
But sometimes in early morning,
or at scented dusk, what I see
and read converge

into a kind of symmetry,
a blending of sight and syllable,
a language as new to me
as the most tropical landscape.
So that when night finally falls
and I lie in the strange dark,
the rustling I think I hear could be
leaves, or wings, or pages turning,
and on the winding road to sleep
I could be anywhere.

The Islands

In paradise, a breeze
blows back our sheets each night
and leaves us almonds
on the pillow;

the volcano smolders
benignly—a sideshow
for our benefit;

we bathe our sins
in waterfalls;

so many flowering
air plants—the breaking
up of rainbows into particles
of blossom;

the prick on the tongue
of pineapple;

the shape of the serpent here
transformed to woven wreaths
of welcome;

and all the time
the surf—a kind of thorough bass,
God's voice beneath
the consciousness
of music.

Back home
we call it jet lag—
this compulsion
of the eyes to close for good
on winter.

Effets de Neige: Impressionists in Winter

The Phillips Collection, Washington DC, 1998

Soaked as they were in the yellow light
of summer, it took the Impressionists years
to venture out into winter
with their brushes and paints.

Monet was first,
in boots and gloves perhaps;
Manet and Sisley followed.
Even Gauguin, lost

in his smoldering dream
of the tropics, wanted to capture
December's merciless
and sparkling light.

So here we are, more
than a hundred years later,
in these rooms of freezing fields, of snow
on houses, snow on haystacks, snow

on barns and railroad tracks.
It is as if the roof of the museum
had opened and a blizzard
had come through the ceiling

covering every canvas in sight
with the frigid instruments
of winter, with a hundred
shades of white.

After a Long Absence, I Return
to a Site of Former Happiness

This is what the world will be
without me, I think, visiting
a place I frequented for twenty years
and finding the same high hills
still straining to be mountains,
the same mowed fields studded
with clover, even the familiar picture shapes
of clouds, like old metaphors
not quite exact enough to trust.

When I visited my childhood home,
ten years after my mother's death,
the rose-encrusted fence
had been stripped away, leaving
the house exposed like a tooth
whose roots are opened
to the painful fact of air,
and there was a kind of satisfaction to that.
It meant that even as I changed

into someone else, the world
was changing too (though
in the dusty attic of memory
the old sewing machine
I stitched my index finger with remains,
as the scar remains despite
its shiny layers of new skin).
But here the narrow road I wander down
winds through my own past

peopled with strangers dressed
in the kind of clothes I wore,
the same bright books tucked
under their arms, as if time were no more
than a colorized film whose actors are interchangeable.
And as I see how easily I'll be replaced on earth,
I think: if there's a poem of affirmation here,
a poem without bitterness or a shadow
of self-pity, then someone else must write it.

5.

The Butterfly Tree

Like tiny Japanese fans, opening
and closing on silent hinges,

a dozen monarchs
and swallowtails hover

over this tree, as if they were
its second crop of blossoms.

Under the leaves, the invisible
hum of bees.

I move away. Such beauty
must be dangerous.

The Death of the Bee

"The death of wild bee populations has become widespread ..."
—news report

The biography of the bee
is written in honey
and is drawing
to a close.

Soon the buzzing
plainchant of summer
will be silenced
for good;

the flowers, unkindled
will blaze
one last time
and go out.

And the boy nursing
his stung ankle this morning
will look back
at his brief tears

with something
like regret,
remembering the amber
taste of honey.

Threshold

There is a hesitation
between seasons

when the last live leaf, for instance,
waits to shrivel

or when spring gathers its green forces
beyond bare branches.

There is no odor
of smoke or lilac;

the sky is no particular color.
But in those brief pauses

we mourn the past
even as we sense the future.

Shy as a girl on the blooded threshold
of being a woman,

we wait, holding our breath,
until the earth stirs

and shakes itself
and the next thing happens.

Fame

There will be no vivid colors
this autumn, because of the drought,
because the loyalties
of weather are changing.

The leaves will bow out
without the usual fanfare,
no curtain calls,
no tide of tourists.

They will simply fade
and fall as we do and,
one day sooner than last year,
be forgotten.

Oak Leaves

are the last to fall,
like afterthoughts
or footnotes
to the season.
From our window
we hardly notice them,
and yet
the trees are entirely
uncovered now.
It is the final
faithlessness.

Poison Ivy

Even then the leaves shone
in green trios, turning
to red in autumn,

a season which in that garden
was simply a quickening of the breeze
for variety's sake.

Pale flowers grew like shadows
of flowers along the stems,
and from these she made bouquets

for their simple table.
Sometimes untangling the vines
from around a tree

she would weave garlands
to wear around her naked neck
or wrists, to please Adam.

Ivy, they named it, a child
of the sumac clan, mild
and innocent of harm as they were.

In the Garden

I tell my dog to sit
and he sits
and I give him
a biscuit.
I tell him to come
and he comes
and sits,
and I give him
a biscuit
again.
I tell my dog Lie Down!
and he sits,
looking up
at me with trust
and adoration.
I pause.
I give him
a biscuit.
This is the beginning
of love and
disobedience.
I was never meant
to be a God.

The Months

January

Contorted by wind,
mere armatures for ice or snow,
the trees resolve
to endure for now,

they will leaf out in April.
And I must be as patient
as the trees—
a winter resolution

I break all over again,
as the cold presses
its sharp blade
against my throat.

February

After endless
hibernation
on the windowsill,
the orchid blooms—

embroidered purple stitches
up and down
a slender stem.
Outside, snow

melts midair
to rain.
Abbreviated month.
Every kind of weather.

March

When the Earl King came
to steal away the child
in Goethe's poem, the father said
don't be afraid,

it's just the wind . . .
As if it weren't the wind
that blows away the tender
fragments of this world—

leftover leaves in the corners
of the garden, a Lenten Rose
that thought it safe
to bloom so early.

April

In the pastel blur
of the garden,
the cherry
and redbud

shake rain
from their delicate
shoulders, as petals
of pink

dogwood
wash down the ditches
in dreamlike
rivers of color.

May

Mayapple, daffodil,
hyacinth, lily,
and by the front
porch steps

every billowing
shade of purple
and lavender lilac,
my mother's favorite flower,

sweet breath drifting through
the open windows:
perfume of memory—conduit
of spring.

June

The June bug
on the screen door
whirs like a small,
ugly machine,

and a chorus of frogs
and crickets drones like Muzak
at all the windows.
What we don't quite see

comforts us.
Blink of lightning, grumble
of thunder—just the heat
clearing its throat.

July

Tonight the fireflies
light their brief
candles
in all the trees

of summer—
color of moonflakes,
color of fluorescent
lace

where the ocean drags
its torn hem
over the dark
sand.

August

Barefoot
and sun-dazed,
I bite into this ripe peach
of a month,

gathering children
into my arms
in all their sandy
splendor,

heaping
my table each night
with nothing
but corn and tomatoes.

September

Their summer romance
over, the lovers
still cling
to each other

the way the green
leaves cling
to their trees
in the strange heat

of September, as if
this time
there will be
no autumn.

October

How suddenly
the woods
have turned
again. I feel

like Daphne, standing
with my arms
outstretched
to the season,

overtaken
by color, crowned
with the hammered gold
of leaves.

November

These anonymous
leaves, their wet
bodies pressed
against the window

or falling past—
I count them
in my sleep,
absolving gravity,

absolving even death
who knows as I do
the imperatives
of the season.

December

The white dove of winter
sheds its first
fine feathers;
they melt

as they touch
the warm ground
like notes
of a once familiar

music; the earth
shivers and
turns towards
the solstice.

4/82

Narragansett Public Library
35 Kingstown Rd
Narragansett, RI 02882